# WORD BIRD'S EASTER WORDS

by Jane Belk Moncure

illustrated by Lois Axeman

Created by

THE CHILD'S WORLD

Distributed by CHILDRENS PRESS ®
Chicago, Illinois

CHILDRENS PRESS HARDCOVER EDITION
ISBN 0-516-06575-0

CHILDRENS PRESS PAPERBACK EDITION
ISBN 0-516-46575-9

**Library of Congress Cataloging in Publication Data**

Moncure, Jane Belk.
　Word Bird's Easter words.

　(Word house words for early birds)
　Summary: Word Bird puts words about Easter in his
word house.
　　1. Vocabulary—Juvenile literature.　2. Easter—
Juvenile literature.　[1. Vocabulary.　2. Easter]
I. Axeman, Lois, ill.　II. Title.　III. Series:
Moncure, Jane Belk.　Word house words for early birds.
PE1449.M5273　1987　　　　428.1　　　　87-13784
ISBN 0-89565-363-X

1 2 3 4 5 6 7 8 9 10 11 12 R 95 94 93 92 91 90 89 88 87

# WORD BIRD'S
# EASTER WORDS

# Word Bird made a...

# word house.

"I will put Easter words
in my house," he said.

# He put in these words—

new life

Easter lily

daffodils

violets

8

tulips

# Easter flowers

ducklings

bunnies

chicks

# Easter pets

# Easter bunny

# Easter eggs

chocolate bunnies

chocolate eggs

# Easter candy

jelly beans

marshmallow chicks

# Easter-egg tree

# Easter puppets

The Easter Bunny

His rabbity ears go flippity-flop
as he fills my basket to the top
with Easter treats for Easter day
Then he hippety-hops
away.

# Easter verse

bunny hop

# Easter baskets

# Easter-egg hunt

# Easter party

# Easter bonnet

# Easter suit

# Easter parade

new life

ducklings

Easter flowers

Easter bunny

Easter lily

Easter eggs

tulips

Easter candy

Easter pets

chicks

jelly beans

ese Easter words with  Word Bird ?

Easter-egg tree

Easter-egg hunt

Easter puppets

Easter party

Easter verse

His rabbity ears go flippity flop

Easter bonnet

bunny hop

Easter suit

Easter baskets

Easter parade

You can make an Easter
word house. You can put
Word Bird's words in your
house and read them too.

Can you think of other Easter
words to put in your word house?